20 best
fun cupcake
recipes

Houghton Mifflin Harcourt
Boston • New York • 2013

Copyright © 2013 by General Mills, Minneapolis, Minnesota. All rights reserved.

For information about permission to reproduce selections from this book, write to Permissions, Houghton Mifflin Harcourt Publishing Company, 215 Park Avenue South, New York, New York 10003.

www.hmhco.com

Cover photo: Frog Cupcakes (page 10)

General Mills
Food Content and Relationship Marketing Director: Geoff Johnson
Food Content Marketing Manager: Susan Klobuchar
Senior Editor: Grace Wells
Kitchen Manager: Ann Stuart
Recipe Development and Testing: Betty Crocker Kitchens
Photography: General Mills Photography Studios and Image Library

Houghton Mifflin Harcourt
Publisher: Natalie Chapman
Editorial Director: Cindy Kitchel
Executive Editor: Anne Ficklen
Associate Editor: Heather Dabah
Managing Editor: Rebecca Springer
Production Editor: Kristi Hart
Cover Design: Chrissy Kurpeski
Book Design: Tai Blanche

ISBN 978-0-544-31479-5
Printed in the United States of America

The Betty Crocker Kitchens seal guarantees success in your kitchen. Every recipe has been tested in America's Most Trusted Kitchens™ to meet our high standards of reliability, easy preparation and great taste.

FIND MORE GREAT IDEAS AT
Betty Crocker.com

Dear Friends,

This new collection of colorful mini books has been put together with you in mind because we know that you love great recipes and enjoy cooking and baking but have a busy lifestyle. So every little book in the series contains just 20 recipes for you to treasure and enjoy. Plus, each book is a single subject designed in a bite-size format just for you—it's easy to use and is filled with favorite recipes from the Betty Crocker Kitchens!

All of the books are conveniently divided into short chapters so you can quickly find what you're looking for, and the beautiful photos throughout are sure to entice you into making the delicious recipes. In the series, you'll discover a fabulous array of recipes to spark your interest—from cookies, cupcakes and birthday cakes to party ideas for a variety of occasions. There's grilled foods, potluck favorites and even gluten-free recipes too.

You'll love the variety in these mini books—so pick one or choose them all for your cooking pleasure.

Enjoy and happy cooking!

Sincerely,

Betty Crocker

contents

Party Cupcakes
Confetti Candy Cupcakes • 6
Game Day Cupcakes • 7
Flower Cupcakes • 8
Star-Studded Celebration Cupcakes • 9

Kids' Cupcakes
Frog Cupcakes • 10
Goin' Fishin' Cupcakes • 11
Chocolate Moose Cupcakes • 12
Dreamy Sleepover Cupcakes • 13
Jungle Animal Cupcakes • 14

Foodie Cupcakes
Hot Chocolate Cupcakes • 15
Root Beer Float Cupcakes • 16
Sunnyside-Up Bacon Cupcakes • 17
Watermelon Slice Cupcakes • 18
Cupcake Sliders • 20

Holiday Cupcakes
New Year's Party Cupcakes • 22
Fireworks Cupcake Towers • 23
Owl and Spider Cupcakes • 24
Thanksgiving Turkey Cupcakes • 25
Snowman Cupcakes • 26
Red Velvet Elf Cupcakes • 27

Metric Conversion Guide • 28
Recipe Testing and Calculating Nutrition
  Information • 29

Party Cupcakes

Confetti Candy Cupcakes

Prep Time: 55 Minutes • **Start to Finish:** 1 Hour 55 Minutes • Makes 30 cupcakes

Cupcakes

- 2⅓ cups Gold Medal® all-purpose flour
- 2½ teaspoons baking powder
- ½ teaspoon salt
- 1 cup butter or margarine, softened
- 1¼ cups granulated sugar
- 3 eggs
- 1 teaspoon vanilla
- ⅔ cup milk
- 1 cup coarsely chopped candy-coated chocolate candies (about 6½ oz)

Frosting

- 1 cup granulated sugar
- ½ cup unsweetened baking cocoa
- ½ cup milk
- ¼ cup butter or margarine
- 2 tablespoons light corn syrup
- 1 teaspoon vanilla
- 1½ to 2 cups powdered sugar

Garnish

Candy-coated chocolate candies (about ¾ cup)

1 Heat oven to 350°F. Place paper baking cup in each of 30 regular-size muffin cups, grease bottoms and sides of muffin cups with shortening and lightly flour, or spray with baking spray with flour.

2 In medium bowl, mix flour, baking powder and salt; set aside.

3 In large bowl, beat 1 cup butter with electric mixer on medium speed 30 seconds. Gradually add granulated sugar, about ¼ cup at a time, beating well after each addition and scraping bowl occasionally. Beat 2 minutes longer. Add eggs, one at a time, beating well after each addition. Beat in 1 teaspoon vanilla. On low speed, alternately add flour mixture, about one-third at a time, and ⅔ cup milk, about half at a time, beating just until blended.

4 Divide batter evenly among muffin cups, filling each with about 3 tablespoons batter or until about two-thirds full. Sprinkle batter in each cup with 1 heaping teaspoon chopped candies.

5 Bake 20 to 25 minutes or until toothpick inserted in center comes out clean. Cool 5 minutes. Remove cupcakes from pans; place on cooling racks. Cool completely, about 30 minutes.

6 In 2-quart saucepan, mix 1 cup granulated sugar and the cocoa. Stir in ½ cup milk, ¼ cup butter and the corn syrup. Heat to boiling over medium-high heat, stirring frequently. Boil 3 minutes, stirring occasionally. Remove from heat; beat in 1 teaspoon vanilla and enough powdered sugar with spoon until frosting is smooth and spreadable. Frost cooled cupcakes. Garnish each with 5 candy-coated chocolate candies.

1 Cupcake: Calories 280; Total Fat 11g (Saturated Fat 7g, Trans Fat 0g); Cholesterol 45mg; Sodium 170mg; Total Carbohydrate 41g (Dietary Fiber 1g); Protein 2g **Exchanges:** 1½ Starch, 1 Other Carbohydrate, 2 Fat **Carbohydrate Choices:** 3

Tip Choose colors of the candy-coated chocolate candies to match the holiday, such as red and green for Christmas.

Game Day Cupcakes

Prep Time: 1 Hour 25 Minutes • **Start to Finish:** 3 Hours • Makes 24 cupcakes

Turn simple chocolate cupcakes into winning cupcakes with simple pretzel and candy game-time decorations.

1 Heat oven to 350°F (325°F for dark or nonstick pans). Place paper baking cup in each of 24 regular-size muffin cups.

2 Make and bake cake mix as directed on box for cupcakes, using water, oil and eggs. Cool 10 minutes. Remove cupcakes from pans; place on cooling racks. Cool completely, about 30 minutes.

3 Divide frosting between 2 small bowls. To create your favorite team colors, add desired food color to each bowl and stir until thoroughly blended.

4 Frost cupcakes; sprinkle with stars. For footballs, pipe laces on almonds with decorating icing. Cut each fruit snack into 6 triangles. Wrap each triangle around 1 end of each pretzel for flag. Decorate each cupcake with 1 football and 1 flag.

Cupcakes

1 box Betty Crocker® SuperMoist® devil's food cake mix

Water, vegetable oil and eggs called for on cake mix box

Frosting

1 container (12 oz) Betty Crocker Whipped fluffy white frosting

Paste food color

Decoration

Star-shaped candy sprinkles

1 tube (4.25 oz) white decorating icing

24 milk chocolate-covered almonds (from 3-oz box)

4 rolls Betty Crocker Fruit by the Foot® chewy fruit snack (any flavor; from 4.5-oz box)

24 thin pretzel sticks

1 Cupcake: Calories 190; Total Fat 7g (Saturated Fat 2g, Trans Fat 1g); Cholesterol 20mg; Sodium 180mg; Total Carbohydrate 29g (Dietary Fiber 1g); Protein 2g **Exchanges:** ½ Starch, 1½ Other Carbohydrate, 1½ Fat **Carbohydrate Choices:** 2

Tip If you have only one pan and a recipe calls for more cupcakes than your pan will make, cover and refrigerate the rest of the batter while baking the first batch. Cool the pan about 15 minutes, then bake the rest of the batter, adding 1 to 2 minutes to the bake time.

Flower Cupcakes

Prep Time: 25 Minutes • **Start to Finish:** 1 Hour 30 Minutes • Makes 24 cupcakes

1 box Betty Crocker SuperMoist white cake mix

Water, vegetable oil and egg whites called for on cake mix box

1 container (1 lb) Betty Crocker Rich & Creamy vanilla or creamy white frosting

30 large marshmallows

Colored candy sprinkles

Birthday candles, if desired

1 Heat oven to 350°F (325°F for dark or nonstick pans).

2 Make, bake and cool cake mix as directed on box for 24 cupcakes. Frost cupcakes.

3 Spray blades of kitchen scissors with cooking spray. Cut each marshmallow crosswise into 4 slices; sprinkle slices with colored sugar. Arrange 5 slices on each cupcake in flower shape. Place candle in center of each flower. Store loosely covered.

1 Cupcake (Cake and Frosting Only): Calories 180; Total Fat 7g (Saturated Fat 1.5g, Trans Fat 1g); Cholesterol 0mg; Sodium 180mg; Total Carbohydrate 28g (Dietary Fiber 0g); Protein 1g **Exchanges:** ½ Starch, 1½ Other Carbohydrate, 1½ Fat **Carbohydrate Choices:** 2

Tip Use edible glitter in place of the colored sugar for extra sparkle. Be sure to checkout party-supply or cake-decorating stores for fun birthday candles.

Star-Studded Celebration Cupcakes

Prep Time: 25 Minutes • **Start to Finish:** 1 Hour 30 Minutes • Makes 36 cupcakes

Garnish

3 (4 oz each) white chocolate baking bars, melted, if desired

1 (4 oz) bar sweet baking chocolate or semisweet baking chocolate

Cupcakes

2 cups Gold Medal all-purpose flour

2 cups sugar

1¼ teaspoons baking soda

1 teaspoon salt

½ teaspoon baking powder

1 cup water

¾ cup sour cream

¼ cup shortening

1 teaspoon vanilla

2 eggs

4 oz unsweetened baking chocolate, melted, cooled

Frosting

1 container Betty Crocker Rich & Creamy white or milk chocolate frosting

1 In medium microwavable bowl, microwave white chocolate baking bars uncovered on Medium (50%) 1½ to 2 minutes. Stir; microwave in 30-second increments, stirring after each, until chocolate is melted and smooth. Pour onto waxed paper–lined cookie sheets. Spread evenly to about ⅛- to ¼-inch thickness. Refrigerate until slightly hardened, about 10 minutes. Repeat with sweet baking chocolate.

2 Lightly sprinkle white chocolate with baking cocoa, if desired. Press small star cutters of desired sizes firmly into chocolate. Lift gently from waxed paper with spatula.

3 Heat oven to 350°F. Place paper baking cup in each of 36 regular-size muffin cups. In large bowl, beat all cupcake ingredients with electric mixer on low speed 30 seconds, scraping bowl constantly. Beat on high speed 3 minutes, scraping bowl occasionally. Divide batter evenly among muffin cups, filling each about half full.

4 Bake 20 to 25 minutes or until toothpick inserted in center comes out clean. Remove cupcakes from pans; place on cooling racks. Cool completely, about 30 minutes.

5 Frost cupcakes. Garnish with chocolate cutouts.

1 Frosted Cupcake (Undecorated): Calories 180; Total Fat 6g (Saturated Fat 2.5g, Trans Fat 1g); Cholesterol 15mg; Sodium 150mg; Total Carbohydrate 29g (Dietary Fiber 0g); Protein 1g **Exchanges:** ½ Starch, 1½ Other Carbohydrate, 1 Fat **Carbohydrate Choices:** 2

Tip Need to save time? Substitute 1 box Betty Crocker SuperMoist devil's food cake mix for the cupcakes above. Make cake mix as directed on box. Frost and decorate cupcakes as directed in recipe. Makes 24 cupcakes.

Kids' Cupcakes

Frog Cupcakes
Prep Time: 25 Minutes • **Start to Finish:** 1 Hour 25 Minutes • Makes 24 cupcakes

1 box Betty Crocker SuperMoist white cake mix

Water, vegetable oil and egg whites called for on cake mix box

2 containers (1 lb each) Betty Crocker Rich & Creamy creamy white frosting

Green gel food color

48 miniature vanilla wafer cookies

48 red cinnamon candies

Red decorating icing (from 4.25-oz tube)

Large red gumdrops

1 Heat oven to 350°F (325°F for dark or nonstick pans). Make, bake and cool cake as directed on box for 24 cupcakes.

2 Reserve 2 tablespoons frosting. Tint remaining frosting with food color; frost cupcakes.

3 For eyes, place 2 cookies near top edge of each cupcake, inserting on end so they stand up. Attach 1 cinnamon candy to each cookie with reserved white frosting. Add dots of white frosting for nostrils.

4 For mouth, pipe on red icing. Slice gumdrops; add slice to each cupcake for tongue. Store loosely covered.

1 Cupcake (Cake and Frosting Only): Calories 250; **Total Fat** 9g (Saturated Fat 2g, Trans Fat 2g); **Cholesterol** 0mg; **Sodium** 220mg; **Total Carbohydrate** 40g (Dietary Fiber 0g); **Protein** 1g **Exchanges:** ½ Starch, 2 Other Carbohydrate, 2 Fat **Carbohydrate Choices:** 2½

Tip For a touch of whimsy, cut small pieces of black gumdrops and place one on each "tongue" to resemble a fly.

Betty Crocker 20 Best Fun Cupcake Recipes

Goin' Fishin' Cupcakes

Prep Time: 1 Hour • **Start to Finish:** 2 Hours 30 Minutes • Makes 24 cupcakes

Cupcakes

1 box Betty Crocker SuperMoist devil's food cake mix

Water, vegetable oil and eggs called for on cake mix box

1 container (1 lb) Betty Crocker Rich & Creamy vanilla or butter cream frosting

Blue gel food color

Fishing Poles

24 cocktail straws

24 pieces dental floss

24 Betty Crocker Shark Bites® chewy fruit snacks (2 to 3 pouches)

1 Heat oven to 350°F (325°F for dark or nonstick pans). Make, bake and cool cake as directed on box for 24 cupcakes.

2 Tint frosting with food color. Frost cupcakes; pull up on frosting, using metal spatula, so frosting looks like waves.

3 To make fishing poles, cut each straw to make one 3-inch piece. Cut dental floss into 3½-inch lengths. Attach piece of dental floss to end of each straw, using needle, to look like fish line. Attach 1 fruit snack to end of each piece of dental floss. Decorate each cupcake with a fishing pole. Store loosely covered.

1 Cupcake (Cake and Frosting Only): Calories 190; Total Fat 9g (Saturated Fat 2g, Trans Fat 1g); Cholesterol 25mg; Sodium 200mg; Total Carbohydrate 28g (Dietary Fiber 0g); Protein 1g **Exchanges:** ½ Starch, 1½ Other Carbohydrate, 1½ Fat **Carbohydrate Choices:** 2

Tip Keep the party theme going by serving blue raspberry punch with "fishy" ice cubes. Place 1 Shark Bites chewy fruit snack in each section of an ice-cube tray. Fill with ginger ale or water, and freeze until solid.

Chocolate Moose Cupcakes

Prep Time: 1 Hour 15 Minutes • **Start to Finish:** 2 Hours 5 Minutes • Makes 14 cupcakes

Cupcakes

1 cup milk

½ cup vegetable oil

1 egg

1½ cups Gold Medal all-purpose flour

¾ cup granulated sugar

⅓ cup unsweetened baking cocoa

1½ teaspoons baking powder

½ teaspoon salt

¾ cup chopped maraschino cherries, well drained

Frosting

½ cup butter or margarine, softened

3 oz unsweetened baking chocolate, melted, cooled

3 cups powdered sugar

2 teaspoons vanilla

3 to 4 tablespoons milk

Decorations

14 peanut-shaped peanut butter sandwich cookies

14 small pretzel twists, cut lengthwise in half

White and red decorating icing (from 6.4-oz cans)

28 blue candy-coated chocolate candies

28 brown candy-coated chocolate candies

1 Heat oven to 375°F. Place paper baking cup in each of 14 regular-size muffin cups, or grease bottoms only of muffin cups with shortening.

2 In medium bowl, beat milk, oil and egg with fork. Stir in remaining cupcake ingredients except cherries just until flour is moistened. Stir in cherries. Divide batter evenly among muffin cups (cups will be almost full).

3 Bake 18 to 20 minutes or until toothpick inserted in center comes out clean. Cool 5 minutes. Remove cupcakes from pan; place on cooling rack. Cool completely, about 30 minutes.

4 In large bowl, mix butter and chocolate. Stir in powdered sugar. Beat in vanilla and milk until smooth and spreadable. If frosting is too thick, beat in more milk, a few drops at a time. If frosting becomes too thin, beat in a small amount of powdered sugar. Place ½ cup frosting in small microwavable bowl. Microwave uncovered on High 5 to 10 seconds or until frosting is melted and can be stirred smooth. Dip tops and sides of peanut butter cookies in melted frosting; place on waxed paper until hardened, about 15 minutes.

5 Frost cupcakes with remaining frosting. Press 1 coated cookie onto each cupcake so cookie extends over edge of cupcake to look like snout of moose. Poke 1 pretzel half into each cupcake, behind cookie, for antlers. Use white decorating icing to pipe eyes and nostrils. Use red decorating icing to pipe mouths. Attach blue candies for eyes and brown candies for ears.

1 Cupcake: Calories 490; Total Fat 21g (Saturated Fat 8g, Trans Fat 0g); Cholesterol 35mg; Sodium 300mg; Total Carbohydrate 70g (Dietary Fiber 2g); Protein 4g **Exchanges:** 1½ Starch, 3 Other Carbohydrate, 4 Fat **Carbohydrate Choices:** 4½

Tip For a fun party idea, make a centerpiece by placing the moose in a circle on a tray.

Dreamy Sleepover Cupcakes

Prep Time: 2 Hours 40 Minutes • **Start to Finish:** 3 Hours 40 Minutes • Makes 24 cupcakes

White Cupcakes

2¾ cups Gold Medal all-purpose flour
3 teaspoons baking powder
½ teaspoon salt
¾ cup shortening
1⅔ cups granulated sugar
5 egg whites
2½ teaspoons vanilla
1¼ cups milk

Frosting

6 cups powdered sugar
⅔ cup butter or margarine, softened
1 tablespoon vanilla
3 to 4 tablespoons milk

Decorations

48 vanilla wafer cookies
Assorted colors decorating icing (from 6.4-oz cans)
12 rolls Betty Crocker Fruit by the Foot chewy fruit snack (any flavor; from two 4.5-oz boxes)
Assorted candy sprinkles, if desired

1 Heat oven to 350°F. Place paper baking cup in each of 24 regular-size muffin cups.

2 In medium bowl, mix flour, baking powder and salt; set aside. In large bowl, beat shortening with electric mixer on medium speed 30 seconds. Gradually add granulated sugar, about ⅓ cup at a time, beating well after each addition. Beat 2 minutes longer. Add egg whites, one at a time, beating well after each addition. Beat in 2½ teaspoons vanilla. On low speed, alternately add flour mixture, about one-third at a time, and milk, about half at a time, beating just until blended.

3 Divide batter evenly among muffin cups, filling each about two-thirds full.

4 Bake 18 to 20 minutes or until toothpick inserted in center comes out clean. Cool 5 minutes. Remove cupcakes from pans; place on cooling racks. Cool completely, about 30 minutes.

5 In large bowl, mix powdered sugar and butter with spoon or electric mixer on low speed. Stir in 1 tablespoon vanilla and 3 tablespoons milk. Gradually beat in just enough remaining milk to make frosting smooth and spreadable. Frost cupcakes.

6 On each cupcake, press 2 vanilla wafers, 1 for the head and 1 for the body. With decorating icing, decorate 1 wafer with eyes, mouth and hair. Cut 4 x 2½-inch pieces from chewy fruit snack; press on cupcakes, covering other cookie, to look like a blanket. Decorate blankets with decorating icing and candy sprinkles.

1 Cupcake: Calories 340; Total Fat 14g (Saturated Fat 8g, Trans Fat 0.5g); Cholesterol 60mg; Sodium 230mg; Total Carbohydrate 50g (Dietary Fiber 0g); Protein 2g **Exchanges:** 1 Starch, 2½ Other Carbohydrate, 2½ Fat **Carbohydrate Choices:** 3

Tip Need to save time? Use 1 box Betty Crocker SuperMoist white, yellow or devil's food cake mix instead of from-scratch cupcakes. Make cake mix as directed on box using water, oil and eggs or egg whites. Bake and cool as directed on box for 24 cupcakes. For the frosting, substitute 1 container (1 lb) Betty Crocker Rich & Creamy vanilla frosting. Decorate cupcakes as directed in recipe.

Jungle Animal Cupcakes

Prep Time: 2 Hours 45 Minutes • **Start to Finish:** 2 Hours 45 Minutes • Makes 24 cupcakes

Cupcakes and Frosting
- 1 box Betty Crocker SuperMoist yellow or devil's food cake mix
- Water, vegetable oil and eggs called for on cake mix box
- 1¼ cups Betty Crocker Rich & Creamy chocolate frosting (from 1-lb container)
- Black food color
- 2½ cups Betty Crocker Rich & Creamy vanilla frosting (from 1-lb container)
- Yellow and red food colors

Lion Decorations
- 1½ cups caramel popcorn
- 12 brown miniature candy-coated chocolate baking bits
- 12 pretzel sticks
- 12 pieces Cheerios® cereal (any flavor)

Tiger Decorations
- 12 brown miniature candy-coated chocolate baking bits
- 12 orange chewy fruit-flavored gumdrops (not sugar coated), cut in half crosswise, top halves discarded

Monkey Decorations
- 12 brown miniature candy-coated chocolate baking bits
- 6 miniature marshmallows, cut in half crosswise, pieces flattened
- 12 small round chocolate-covered creamy mints

Zebra Decorations
- 6 round vanilla wafer cookies
- 24 brown miniature candy-coated chocolate baking bits
- 6 black chewy licorice-flavored gumdrops (not sugar coated), cut in half vertically

1 Heat oven to 350°F (325°F for dark or nonstick pans). Place paper baking cup in each of 24 regular-size muffin cups. Make and bake cake mix as directed on box for 24 cupcakes. Cool 10 minutes. Remove cupcakes from pans; place on cooling rack. Cool completely, about 30 minutes. Decorate cupcakes to make 6 lions, 6 tigers, 6 monkeys and 6 zebras.

2 In small bowl, mix ½ cup chocolate frosting with black food color to make black frosting. Place in resealable food-storage plastic bag; cut small tip off 1 corner of bag. Use black frosting to decorate lions, tigers, monkeys and zebras (steps 3 through 7).

3 Lions and Tigers: In medium bowl, mix 1 cup vanilla frosting with enough yellow and red food colors to make orange. In small bowl, mix 1 tablespoon orange frosting with 3 tablespoons white vanilla frosting to make lighter orange for muzzles. Frost 12 cupcakes with darker orange frosting. For muzzle, spread or pipe small circle of lighter orange frosting on each cupcake.

4 For lions, place caramel corn around edge of cupcake for mane. For eyes, add brown baking bits. For whiskers, break about ½-inch pieces off each end of pretzel sticks and insert in cupcake. For ears, add cereal pieces. Using black frosting, pipe on mouth and nose.

5 For tigers, use black frosting to pipe on stripes, nose and mouth. For eyes, add brown baking bits. For ears, add gumdrop halves.

6 Monkeys: Frost 6 cupcakes with chocolate frosting. In small bowl, mix 1 tablespoon chocolate frosting and 2 tablespoons vanilla frosting to make light brown. For muzzle, spread or pipe circle of light brown on each cupcake that starts in middle and extends to edge; pipe small tuft of hair on opposite edge. For each eye, attach brown baking bit to marshmallow half with frosting; place on cupcake. With black frosting, pipe on nose and mouth. For ears, add mints.

7 Zebras: Cut small horizontal slit in top of each of 6 cupcakes near edge of paper cup. Insert edge of vanilla wafer cookie into each slit to create elongated face, adding small amount of vanilla frosting to cookie before inserting to help it stick. Frost cupcakes with vanilla frosting. For muzzle, frost cookie with black frosting. With black frosting, pipe on stripes and mane. Add brown baking bits for nostril and eyes. For ears, add black gumdrop halves, cut side down. Store loosely covered.

1 Cupcake (Cake and Frosting Only): Calories 290; Total Fat 12g (Saturated Fat 3g, Trans Fat 2.5g); Cholesterol 25mg; Sodium 240mg; Total Carbohydrate 43g (Dietary Fiber 0g); Protein 1g **Exchanges:** ½ Starch, 2½ Other Carbohydrate, 2½ Fat **Carbohydrate Choices:** 3

Foodie Cupcakes

Hot Chocolate Cupcakes

Prep Time: 20 Minutes • **Start to Finish:** 1 Hour 25 Minutes • Makes 12 cupcakes

- ½ box Betty Crocker SuperMoist devil's food cake mix (about 1⅔ cups)
- ½ cup water
- ¼ cup vegetable oil
- 1 egg
- 1 cup Betty Crocker Whipped vanilla frosting (from 12-oz container)
- ½ cup marshmallow creme
- ¼ teaspoon unsweetened baking cocoa
- 6 miniature pretzel twists, broken in half

1 Heat oven to 350°F (325°F for dark or nonstick pans). Place paper baking cup in each of 12 regular-size muffin cups.

2 In large bowl, beat cake mix, water, oil and egg with electric mixer on low speed 30 seconds, then on medium speed 2 minutes, scraping bowl occasionally. Divide batter evenly among muffin cups.

3 Bake 17 to 22 minutes or until toothpick inserted in center comes out clean. Cool 10 minutes. Remove cupcakes from pan; place on cooling rack. Cool completely, about 30 minutes.

4 In small bowl, mix frosting and marshmallow creme. Spoon into small resealable food-storage plastic bag; seal bag. Cut ⅜-inch tip off 1 corner of bag. (Or spoon mixture onto cupcakes instead of piping.)

5 Pipe 3 small dollops of frosting mixture on top of each cupcake to look like melted marshmallows. Sprinkle with cocoa. Press pretzel half into side of each cupcake for cup handle. Store loosely covered.

1 Cupcake: Calories 200; Total Fat 9g (Saturated Fat 2.5g, Trans Fat 1g); Cholesterol 20mg; Sodium 180mg; Total Carbohydrate 28g (Dietary Fiber 0g); Protein 1g **Exchanges:** ½ Starch, 1½ Other Carbohydrate, 1½ Fat **Carbohydrate Choices:** 2

Tip If you like peppermint, frost these fun cupcakes with the frosting mixture, and sprinkle the tops with crushed candy canes.

Root Beer Float Cupcakes

Prep Time: 1 Hour • **Start to Finish:** 2 Hours • Makes 23 cupcakes

Cupcakes

23 flat-bottom ice cream cones

2⅓ cups Gold Medal all-purpose flour

2½ teaspoons baking powder

½ teaspoon salt

1 cup butter or margarine, softened

1¼ cups granulated sugar

3 whole eggs

1 teaspoon vanilla

⅔ cup milk

⅔ cup root beer (measure liquid only—not foam)

Root beer candies, coarsely crushed, if desired

46 straws, if desired

Fluffy Root Beer Frosting

¾ cup granulated sugar

¾ cup packed brown sugar

⅓ cup cold root beer

¼ cup cream of tartar

Dash salt

2 egg whites

1 teaspoon vanilla

1 Heat oven to 350°F. Stand ice cream cones in muffin pans. In medium bowl, mix flour, baking powder and ½ teaspoon salt; set aside.

2 In large bowl, beat butter with electric mixer on medium speed 30 seconds. Gradually add granulated sugar, about ¼ cup at a time, beating well after each addition and scraping bowl occasionally. Beat 2 minutes longer. Add whole eggs, one at a time, beating well after each addition. Beat in 1 teaspoon vanilla. On low speed, alternately add flour mixture, about one-third a time, and ⅔ cup root beer, about half at a time, beating just until blended.

3 Divide batter evenly among ice cream cones, filling each with scant ¼ cup batter.

4 Bake 20 to 25 minutes or until toothpick inserted in center of cupcake comes out clean. Cool 5 minutes. Remove cones from pans; place on cooling racks. Cool completely, about 30 minutes.

5 In heavy 3-quart saucepan, mix all frosting ingredients except vanilla. Beat with electric mixer on high speed 1 minute, scraping pan constantly. Place over low heat. Beat on high speed about 10 minutes or until stiff peaks form; remove from heat. Add 1 teaspoon vanilla. Beat on high speed 2 minutes or until fluffy.

6 Frost cupcakes; decorate with root beer candies. Cut about 4 inches off bottom of each straw; discard. Poke 2 straws into each cupcake.

1 Cupcake: Calories 250; Total Fat 9g (Saturated Fat 5g, Trans Fat 0g); Cholesterol 50mg; Sodium 220mg; Total Carbohydrate 39g (Dietary Fiber 0g); Protein 3g **Exchanges:** 1½ Starch, 1 Other Carbohydrate, 1½ Fat **Carbohydrate Choices:** 2½

Tip If you want to add a little color, top the frosted cupcakes with colored candy sprinkles.

Sunnyside-Up Bacon Cupcakes

Prep Time: 50 Minutes • **Start to Finish:** 1 Hour 50 Minutes • Makes 24 cupcakes

Cupcakes

2⅓ cups Gold Medal all-purpose flour

2½ teaspoons baking powder

½ teaspoon salt

½ teaspoon ground cinnamon

1 cup butter or margarine, softened

1 cup granulated sugar

3 eggs

2 tablespoons maple-flavored syrup

1 teaspoon vanilla

1 cup milk

¾ cup crumbled crisply cooked maple-flavored bacon (9 slices)

Frosting

6 cups powdered sugar

⅔ cup butter or margarine, softened

1 tablespoon vanilla

3 to 4 tablespoons milk

Decorations

24 butterscotch candies, unwrapped

Black decorator sugar, if desired

1 Heat oven to 350°F. Place paper baking cup in each of 24 regular-size muffin cups.

2 In medium bowl, mix flour, baking powder, salt and cinnamon; set aside. In large bowl, beat 1 cup butter with electric mixer on medium speed 30 seconds. Gradually add granulated sugar, about ¼ cup at a time, beating well after each addition. Beat 2 minutes longer. Add eggs, one at a time, beating well after each addition. Beat in syrup and 1 teaspoon vanilla. On low speed, alternately add flour mixture, about one-third at a time, and milk, about half at a time, beating just until blended.

3 Fold in bacon. Divide batter evenly among muffin cups, filling each about two-thirds full.

4 Bake 20 to 25 minutes or until golden brown and toothpick inserted in center comes out clean. Cool 5 minutes. Remove cupcakes from pans; place on cooling racks. Cool completely, about 30 minutes.

5 In large bowl, beat powdered sugar and ⅔ cup butter with spoon or electric mixer on low speed. Stir in 1 tablespoon vanilla and 3 tablespoons milk. Gradually beat in just enough remaining milk to make frosting smooth and spreadable.

6 Frost cupcakes to look like the white of a sunnyside up egg. For "yolk," press 1 butterscotch candy in center of each cupcake. Sprinkle with black decorator sugar for "pepper."

1 Cupcake: Calories 370; Total Fat 15g (Saturated Fat 9g, Trans Fat 0.5g); Cholesterol 65mg; Sodium 300mg; Total Carbohydrate 55g (Dietary Fiber 0g); Protein 3g **Exchanges:** 1 Starch, 2½ Other Carbohydrate, 3 Fat **Carbohydrate Choices:** 3½

Tip Short on time? Use 1 container (1 lb) Betty Crocker Rich & Creamy vanilla frosting instead of the vanilla buttercream frosting.

Watermelon Slice Cupcakes

Prep Time: 1 Hour 5 Minutes • **Start to Finish:** 2 Hours • Makes 24 cupcakes

Cupcakes

- 2⅓ cups Gold Medal all-purpose flour
- 1 package (0.3 oz) cherry-flavored or other red unsweetened soft drink mix
- 2½ teaspoons baking powder
- ½ teaspoon salt
- 1 cup butter or margarine, softened
- 1¼ cups granulated sugar
- 3 eggs
- 1 teaspoon vanilla
- ⅔ cup pureed watermelon (about 1½ cups watermelon pieces)
- ¾ cup miniature semisweet chocolate chips

Frosting

- ½ cup butter or margarine, softened
- ¼ cup shortening
- 1 teaspoon vanilla
- ⅛ teaspoon salt
- 4 cups powdered sugar
- 2 to 4 tablespoons milk or water
- Green and red paste food color

Decoration

- ¼ cup miniature semisweet chocolate chips

1 Heat oven to 350°F. Place paper baking cup in each of 24 regular-size muffin cups.

2 In medium bowl, mix flour, drink mix, baking powder and ½ teaspoon salt; set aside. In large bowl, beat 1 cup butter with electric mixer on medium speed 30 seconds. Gradually add granulated sugar, about ¼ cup at a time, beating well after each addition. Beat 2 minutes longer. Add eggs, one at a time, beating well after each addition. Beat in 1 teaspoon vanilla. On low speed, alternately add flour mixture, about one-third at a time, and watermelon puree, about half at a time, beating just until blended.

3 Fold in ¾ cup chocolate chips. Divide batter evenly among muffin cups, filling each about two-thirds full.

4 Bake 20 to 25 minutes or until golden brown and toothpick inserted in center comes out clean. Cool 5 minutes. Remove cupcakes from pans; place on cooling racks. Cool completely, about 30 minutes.

5 In large bowl, beat ½ cup butter and the shortening with electric mixer on medium speed until light and fluffy. Beat in 1 teaspoon vanilla and ⅛ teaspoon salt. On low speed, beat in powdered sugar, 1 cup at a time, scraping down sides of bowl occasionally. Add 2 tablespoons milk; beat on high speed until light and fluffy. Gradually beat in just enough remaining milk to make frosting smooth and spreadable.

6 Tint 1 cup frosting with green food color. Place green frosting in decorating bag fitted with star tip #19; set aside. Tint remaining frosting with red food color. Frost cooled cupcakes with red frosting to within ½ inch of edge. Pipe 1 row of green frosting around edge of each cupcake to look like watermelon rind. Decorate each with chocolate chips to look like seeds.

1 Cupcake: Calories 340; Total Fat 16g (Saturated Fat 9g, Trans Fat 1g); Cholesterol 55mg; Sodium 240mg; Total Carbohydrate 45g (Dietary Fiber 0g); Protein 2g **Exchanges:** 1 Starch, 2 Other Carbohydrate, 3 Fat **Carbohydrate Choices:** 3

Mini Cupcakes: To make mini cupcakes, place mini paper baking cup in each of 24 mini muffin cups. Make batter as directed in recipe. Fill each cup with about 1 tablespoon plus 1 teaspoon batter or until about two-thirds full. (Cover and refrigerate remaining batter until ready to bake; cool pan 15 minutes before reusing.) Bake 17 to 20 minutes or until golden brown and toothpick inserted in center comes out clean. Cool 5 minutes. Remove cupcakes from pans; place on cooling racks. Cool completely, about 15 minutes. Repeat with remaining batter to make an additional 48 mini cupcakes. Frost as directed. Makes 72 mini cupcakes.

Tip When mixing the green frosting, don't completely mix in the green food color so that the frosting remains white in some parts. Then, when it's piped onto the cupcakes, it will more accurately resemble the rind of a watermelon.

Cupcake Sliders

Prep Time: 1 Hour 40 Minutes • **Start to Finish:** 3 Hours 20 Minutes • Makes 64 cupcake sliders

Cupcakes

- 2⅓ cups Gold Medal all-purpose flour
- 2½ teaspoons baking powder
- ½ teaspoon salt
- 1 cup butter or margarine, softened
- 1¼ cups sugar
- 3 eggs
- 1 teaspoon vanilla
- ⅔ cup milk

Brownies

- 1 box (1 lb 2.3 oz) Betty Crocker fudge brownie mix
- ¼ cup water
- ⅔ cup vegetable oil
- 2 eggs

Toppings

- 1½ cups flaked coconut
- 4 to 6 drops green food color
- 4 to 6 drops water
- 1 cup Betty Crocker Rich & Creamy chocolate frosting (from 1-lb container)
- 64 orange juicy chewy fruit candies, unwrapped
- 16 rolls Betty Crocker Fruit by the Foot strawberry chewy fruit snack (from three 4.5-oz boxes), unwrapped
- 2 tablespoons honey
- 1 to 2 teaspoons water
- 2 tablespoons sesame seed

1 Heat oven to 350°F. Place mini paper baking cup in each of 24 mini muffin cups. In medium bowl, mix flour, baking powder and salt; set aside.

2 In large bowl, beat butter with electric mixer on medium speed 30 seconds. Gradually add sugar, about ¼ cup at a time, beating well after each addition. Beat 2 minutes longer. Add 3 eggs, one at a time, beating well after each addition. Beat in vanilla. On low speed, alternately add flour mixture, about one-third at a time, and milk, about half at a time, beating just until blended.

3 Fill each cup with about 1 tablespoon plus 1 teaspoon batter or until about two-thirds full. (Cover and refrigerate remaining batter until ready to bake; cool pan 15 minutes before reusing.) Bake 17 to 20 minutes or until golden brown and toothpick inserted in center comes out clean. Cool 5 minutes. Remove cupcakes from pans; place on cooling racks. Cool completely, about 15 minutes. Repeat with remaining batter to make an additional 48 mini cupcakes.

4 Leave oven temperature at 350°F. Grease 15 x 10 x 1-inch pan with shortening or cooking spray. In large bowl, stir brownie mix, ¼ cup water, the oil and 2 eggs with spoon until blended. Pour into pan. Bake 22 to 26 minutes or until toothpick inserted 2 inches from edge comes out almost clean. Cool 20 minutes. With 1½-inch round cutter, cut 64 brownie rounds for "burgers."

5 In medium bowl, toss coconut, green food color and 4 to 6 drops water with fork until coconut reaches desired color; set aside.

6 Remove paper baking cups from 64 cupcakes (reserve remaining cupcakes for another use). Cut each cupcake crosswise into halves to make tops and bottoms of "buns." Place brownie rounds (burgers) on bottom halves of cupcakes (buns), using frosting to secure.

7 To make "cheese slices," on large microwavable plate, microwave about 8 chewy fruit candies at a time on High 5 to 10 seconds to soften. Use bottom of measuring cup to flatten until each is about 1¾ inches in diameter. Secure to "burgers" with frosting. Repeat to make additional "cheese slices."

8 To make "ketchup," cut chewy fruit snack with kitchen scissors into about 1¾-inch irregular-edged circles. Secure to "cheese" with frosting. Spread dab of frosting on "ketchup"; sprinkle each slider with scant 2 teaspoons tinted coconut for "shredded lettuce."

9 In small bowl, mix honey and enough of the 1 to 2 teaspoons water until thin consistency. Brush honey mixture lightly over "bun tops"; sprinkle each with sesame seed. Spread dab of frosting on cut sides of "bun tops"; secure to coconut, frosting side down.

1 Cupcake Slider: Calories 190; Total Fat 8g (Saturated Fat 3.5g, Trans Fat 0g); Cholesterol 25mg; Sodium 135mg; Total Carbohydrate 27g (Dietary Fiber 0g); Protein 1g **Exchanges:** ½ Starch, 1½ Other Carbohydrate, 1½ Fat **Carbohydrate Choices:** 2

Tip Brownies can be baked ahead, but wait to cut out the "burgers" until you're ready to assemble them so they don't dry out.

Holiday Cupcakes

New Year's Party Cupcakes

Prep Time: 2 Hours 5 Minutes • **Start to Finish:** 3 Hours 15 Minutes • Makes 28 cupcakes

Cupcakes

2⅓ cups Gold Medal all-purpose flour

2½ teaspoons baking powder

½ teaspoon salt

1 cup butter or margarine, softened

1¼ cups sugar

3 eggs

1 teaspoon vanilla

⅔ cup milk

Decoration

1 bag (12 oz) semisweet chocolate chips (2 cups)

2 teaspoons shortening

24 sample-size ice cream cones (about 1 inch wide at opening and 2½ inches long)

24 frilled toothpicks

Frosting and Icing

6 cups powdered sugar

⅔ cup butter or margarine, softened

1 tablespoon vanilla

3 to 4 tablespoons milk

White decorating icing (from 6.4-oz can)

1 Heat oven to 350°F. Place paper baking cup in each of 24 regular-size muffin cups. Grease and flour muffin cups, or spray with baking spray with flour.

2 In medium bowl, mix flour, baking powder and salt; set aside.

3 In large bowl, beat 1 cup butter with electric mixer on medium speed 30 seconds. Gradually add sugar, about ¼ cup at a time, beating well after each addition and scraping bowl occasionally. Beat 2 minutes longer. Add eggs, one at a time, beating well after each addition. Beat in 1 teaspoon vanilla. On low speed, alternately add flour mixture, about one-third at a time, and milk, about half at a time, beating just until blended.

4 Divide batter evenly among muffin cups, filling each with about 3 tablespoons batter or until about two-thirds full.

5 Bake 20 to 25 minutes or until golden brown and toothpick inserted in center comes out clean. Cool 5 minutes. Remove cupcakes from pans; place on cooling racks to cool.

6 Meanwhile, in small microwavable bowl, microwave chocolate chips and shortening uncovered on High 30 seconds. Stir; microwave about 30 seconds longer or just until mixture can be stirred smooth. Cool slightly. Dip ice cream cones in melted chocolate to coat; wipe off excess. Place point side up on waxed paper–lined plate; insert frilled toothpick into point of each cone. Refrigerate while frosting cupcakes.

7 In large bowl, mix powdered sugar and ⅔ cup butter with spoon or electric mixer on low speed. Stir in 1 tablespoon vanilla and 3 tablespoons of the milk. Gradually beat in just enough remaining milk to make frosting smooth and spreadable. If frosting is too thick, beat in more milk, a few drops at a time. If frosting becomes too thin, beat in a small amount of powdered sugar. Frost cupcakes.

8 Use decorating icing to decorate chocolate-coated cones. Place 1 cone upside down on each cupcake. With decorating icing add "fringe" to edge of cone to look like party hat.

1 Cupcake: Calories 420; Total Fat 19g (Saturated Fat 11g, Trans Fat 0.5g); Cholesterol 60mg; Sodium 230mg; Total Carbohydrate 61g (Dietary Fiber 1g); Protein 3g **Exchanges:** 1 Starch, 3 Other Carbohydrate, 3½ Fat **Carbohydrate Choices:** 4

Tip Short on time? Substitute 1 box yellow cake mix for the yellow cupcakes. Make cake mix as directed on box for cupcakes. For the frosting, substitute 1 container (1 lb) Betty Crocker Rich & Creamy vanilla frosting. Decorate as directed in recipe.

Fireworks Cupcake Towers

Prep Time: 1 Hour 15 Minutes • **Start to Finish:** 2 Hours 35 Minutes • Makes 18 cupcake towers

Cupcakes

2⅓ cups Gold Medal all-purpose flour

2½ teaspoons baking powder

½ teaspoon salt

1 cup butter or margarine, softened

1¼ cups granulated sugar

3 eggs

1 teaspoon vanilla

⅔ cup milk

Icing and Decorations

6 cups powdered sugar

⅔ cup butter or margarine, softened

1 teaspoon vanilla

3 to 4 tablespoons milk

Red and blue paste food color

Red, white and blue candy sprinkles, if desired

Candies and other decors, if desired

1 Heat oven to 350°F. Place paper baking cup in each of 18 regular-size muffin cups and mini paper baking cup in each of 18 mini muffin cups.

2 In medium bowl, mix flour, baking powder and salt; set aside. In large bowl, beat 1 cup butter with electric mixer on medium speed 30 seconds. Gradually add granulated sugar, about ¼ cup at a time, beating well after each addition. Beat 2 minutes longer. Add eggs, one at a time, beating well after each addition. Beat in 1 teaspoon vanilla. On low speed, alternately add flour mixture, about one-third at a time, and milk, about half at a time, beating just until blended.

3 Divide batter evenly among muffin cups, filling each about two-thirds full.

4 Bake regular cupcakes 18 to 25 minutes, mini cupcakes 12 to 20 minutes, or until toothpick inserted in center comes out clean. Cool 5 minutes. Remove cupcakes from pans; place on cooling racks. Cool completely, about 30 minutes.

5 In large bowl, mix powdered sugar and ⅔ cup butter with spoon or electric mixer on low speed. Stir in 1 tablespoon vanilla and 3 teaspoons of the milk. Gradually beat in just enough remaining milk to make frosting smooth and spreadable.

6 Place 1½ cups icing in decorating bag fitted with small round tip (#22). Frost each cupcake (regular and mini) with scant 1 tablespoon icing. Divide remaining icing between 2 bowls; tint icing in 1 bowl red and the other blue.

7 Remove paper liners from mini cupcakes, if desired. Place 1 mini cupcake on top of each regular cupcake. Pipe blue and red icings around base of mini cupcakes (on regular cupcakes) and on top of mini cupcakes, making various length streamers. Use any remaining white icing to fill in streamers between red and blue ones. Sprinkle with candy sprinkles and other decors.

1 Cupcake Tower: Calories 450; Total Fat 18g (Saturated Fat 11g, Trans Fat 0.5g); Cholesterol 80mg; Sodium 310mg; Total Carbohydrate 67g (Dietary Fiber 0g); Protein 3g **Exchanges:** 1 Starch, 3½ Other Carbohydrate, 3½ Fat **Carbohydrate Choices:** 4½

Tip Make the cupcake towers into a centerpiece for your July 4th party. Add to the patriotic theme with plates, napkins and party decor to set the mood!

Owl and Spider Cupcakes

Prep Time: 25 Minutes • **Start to Finish:** 2 Hours 10 Minutes • Makes 24 cupcakes

Cupcakes

1 box Betty Crocker SuperMoist yellow cake mix (or other flavor)

Water, vegetable oil and eggs called for on cake mix box

Frosting and Decorations

Black string licorice, cut into 2-inch pieces

2 containers (1 lb each) Betty Crocker Rich & Creamy chocolate frosting

Black decorator sugar crystals

Large black gumdrops

Red cinnamon candies

Assorted candies

Chocolate wafer cookies

1 Heat oven to 350°F (325°F for dark or nonstick pans). Place paper baking cup in each of 24 regular-size muffin cups.

2 Mix and bake cake mix as directed on box for 24 cupcakes. Cool 10 minutes. Remove cupcakes from pan; place on cooling rack. Cool completely, about 30 minutes.

3 To make spiders, press 4 licorice pieces into each side of 12 of the cupcakes, letting about 1½ inches hang over side of cupcake. Spread tops of cupcakes with chocolate frosting; sprinkle with black decorator sugar crystals. Slice black gumdrops in half for faces. Press red cinnamon candies in center for eyes.

4 To make owls, spread chocolate frosting on remaining 12 cupcakes. Use candies to form eyes, beaks and feet on each cupcake. Cut chocolate wafer cookies into quarters; place wafer pieces, triangle points up, behind eyes for ears. Cut wafer cookies into thirds for wings; place on cupcakes. Store loosely covered.

1 Cupcake (Cake and Frosting Only): Calories 260; Total Fat 10g (Saturated Fat 3g, Trans Fat 2g); Cholesterol 25mg; Sodium 250mg; Total Carbohydrate 40g (Dietary Fiber 0g); Protein 1g **Exchanges:** ½ Starch, 2 Other Carbohydrate, 2 Fat **Carbohydrate Choices:** 2½

Tip Candy corn pieces can be used for the owls' beaks, and yellow ring-shaped hard candies can be used for the eyes.

Thanksgiving Turkey Cupcakes

Prep Time: 45 Minutes • **Start to Finish:** 1 Hour 55 Minutes • Makes 24 cupcakes

1 box Betty Crocker SuperMoist yellow cake mix

1¼ cups water

¼ cup vegetable oil

3 eggs

¾ cup creamy peanut butter

1 container (1 lb) Betty Crocker Rich & Creamy chocolate frosting

4 oz vanilla-flavored candy coating (almond bark)

4 oz semisweet baking chocolate

24 Hershey's® Kisses® Brand milk chocolates, unwrapped*

1 Heat oven to 350°F (325°F for dark or nonstick pans). Place paper baking cup in each of 24 regular-size muffin cups.

2 In large bowl, beat cake mix, water, oil, eggs and peanut butter with electric mixer on low speed 30 seconds, then on medium speed 2 minutes, scraping bowl occasionally. Divide batter evenly among muffin cups or until about two-thirds full.

3 Bake 18 to 23 minutes or until toothpick inserted in center comes out clean. Cool 10 minutes. Remove cupcakes from pans; place on cooling rack. Cool completely, about 30 minutes. Frost cupcakes.

4 Line cookie sheet with waxed paper or cooking parchment paper. In separate small microwavable bowls, microwave candy coating and baking chocolate uncovered on High 30 to 60 seconds, stirring every 15 seconds, until melted and smooth. Place coating and chocolate in separate resealable food-storage plastic bags; snip off tiny corner of each bag. Pipe coating and chocolate into feather shapes, about 3 inches long and 2½ inches wide (see photo). Refrigerate coating and chocolate about 5 minutes or until set.

5 When set, peel feathers off waxed paper and insert into cupcakes. Place milk chocolate candy on each cupcake for head of turkey. Store loosely covered.

The HERSHEY'S® KISSES® trademark and trade dress and the Conical figure and plume device are used under license.

1 Cupcake: Calories 300; Total Fat 16g (Saturated Fat 6g, Trans Fat 1g); Cholesterol 30mg; Sodium 230mg; Total Carbohydrate 35g (Dietary Fiber 1g); Protein 4g **Exchanges:** 1½ Starch, 1 Other Carbohydrate, 3 Fat **Carbohydrate Choices:** 2

Tip To make the turkey feathers even more colorful, stir a small amount of red and yellow food color into the melted white candy coating to make it orange.

Holiday Cupcakes

Snowman Cupcakes

Prep Time: 45 Minutes • **Start to Finish:** 2 Hours • Makes 24 cupcakes

- 1 box Betty Crocker SuperMoist white cake mix
- Water, vegetable oil and egg whites called for on cake mix box
- 1 container (12 oz) Betty Crocker Whipped fluffy white frosting
- White decorator sugar crystals
- 1 bag (16 oz) large marshmallows
- Pretzel sticks
- Betty Crocker Fruit by the Foot chewy fruit snack rolls, any red or orange flavor
- Assorted candies (such as gumdrops, gummy ring candies, peppermint candies, chocolate chips, pastel mint chips, candy decors, string licorice)

1 Heat oven to 350°F (325°F for dark or nonstick pans). Make, bake and cool cake mix as directed on box for 24 cupcakes.

2 Set aside ¼ cup frosting. Frost cupcakes with remaining frosting. Sprinkle frosting with sugar crystals. Stack 2 or 3 marshmallows on each cupcake, using ½ teaspoon frosting between marshmallows to attach.

3 For arms, break pretzel sticks into pieces 1½ inches long. Press 2 pieces into 1 marshmallow on each cupcake. Cut 1-inch mitten shapes from fruit snack. Attach mittens to pretzels. For scarf, cut fruit snack into 6 x ¼-inch piece; wrap and tie around base of top marshmallow. For hat, stack candies, using frosting to attach. For earmuff, use piece of string licorice and candies, using frosting to attach. For faces and buttons, attach desired candies with small amount of frosting. Store loosely covered.

1 Cupcake (Cake and Frosting Only): Calories 160; **Total Fat** 7g (Saturated Fat 2g, Trans Fat 1g); **Cholesterol** 0mg; **Sodium** 160mg; **Total Carbohydrate** 24g (Dietary Fiber 0g); **Protein** 1g **Exchanges:** ½ Starch, 1 Other Carbohydrate, 1½ Fat **Carbohydrate Choices:** 1½

Red Velvet Elf Cupcakes

Prep Time: 40 Minutes • **Start to Finish:** 2 Hours 20 Minutes • Makes 24 cupcakes

Cupcakes

- 1 box Betty Crocker SuperMoist German chocolate cake mix
- 1 cup water
- ½ cup vegetable oil
- 3 eggs
- 2 tablespoons unsweetened baking cocoa
- 1 bottle (1 oz) red food color

Frosting and Decorations

- 1 container (1 lb) Betty Crocker Rich & Creamy cream cheese frosting
- 6 dried apricots halves
- 6 rolls Betty Crocker Fruit Roll-Ups® chewy fruit snack, any flavor (from 5-oz box)
- 24 small red gumdrops, cut in half
- 48 semisweet chocolate chips
- 1 pouch (7 oz) red decorating cookie icing

1 Heat oven to 350°F (325°F for dark or nonstick pans). Place paper baking cup in each of 24 regular-size muffin cups.

2 In large bowl, beat all cupcake ingredients with electric mixer on low speed 30 seconds, then on medium speed 2 minutes, scraping bowl occasionally. Divide batter evenly among muffin cups, filling each about two-thirds full.

3 Bake and cool completely as directed on box for cupcakes.

4 Frost cupcakes with frosting, reserving 1 tablespoon frosting. Cut each apricot into 4 pieces; place 2 pieces on each side of cupcakes for ears. Cut each fruit snack into 4 triangles. Place 1 triangle on top of each cupcake, folding pointed end over to form hat. Attach 1 gumdrop half to pointed end of each hat using reserved frosting. Use remaining gumdrop halves for nose and chocolate chips for eyes. Pipe mouth with red cookie icing. Store loosely covered.

1 Cupcake (Cake and Frosting Only): Calories 190; **Total Fat** 10g (Saturated Fat 1.5g, Trans Fat 1g); Cholesterol 25mg; Sodium 85mg; Total Carbohydrate 25g (Dietary Fiber 0g); Protein 1g **Exchanges:** 1½ Other Carbohydrate, 2 Fat **Carbohydrate Choices:** 1½

Tip SuperMoist devil's food cake mix can also be used for dark red velvet cupcakes; omit the cocoa.

Metric Conversion Guide

Volume

U.S. Units	Canadian Metric	Australian Metric
¼ teaspoon	1 mL	1 ml
½ teaspoon	2 mL	2 ml
1 teaspoon	5 mL	5 ml
1 tablespoon	15 mL	20 ml
¼ cup	50 mL	60 ml
⅓ cup	75 mL	80 ml
½ cup	125 mL	125 ml
⅔ cup	150 mL	170 ml
¾ cup	175 mL	190 ml
1 cup	250 mL	250 ml
1 quart	1 liter	1 liter
1½ quarts	1.5 liters	1.5 liters
2 quarts	2 liters	2 liters
2½ quarts	2.5 liters	2.5 liters
3 quarts	3 liters	3 liters
4 quarts	4 liters	4 liters

Weight

U.S. Units	Canadian Metric	Australian Metric
1 ounce	30 grams	30 grams
2 ounces	55 grams	60 grams
3 ounces	85 grams	90 grams
4 ounces (¼ pound)	115 grams	125 grams
8 ounces (½ pound)	225 grams	225 grams
16 ounces (1 pound)	455 grams	500 grams
1 pound	455 grams	0.5 kilogram

Note: The recipes in this cookbook have not been developed or tested using metric measures. When converting recipes to metric, some variations in quality may be noted.

Measurements

Inches	Centimeters
1	2.5
2	5.0
3	7.5
4	10.0
5	12.5
6	15.0
7	17.5
8	20.5
9	23.0
10	25.5
11	28.0
12	30.5
13	33.0

Temperatures

Fahrenheit	Celsius
32°	0°
212°	100°
250°	120°
275°	140°
300°	150°
325°	160°
350°	180°
375°	190°
400°	200°
425°	220°
450°	230°
475°	240°
500°	260°

Recipe Testing and Calculating Nutrition Information

Recipe Testing:

- Large eggs and 2% milk were used unless otherwise indicated.
- Fat-free, low-fat, low-sodium or lite products were not used unless indicated.
- No nonstick cookware and bakeware were used unless otherwise indicated. No dark-colored, black or insulated bakeware was used.
- When a pan is specified, a metal pan was used; a baking dish or pie plate means ovenproof glass was used.
- An electric hand mixer was used for mixing only when mixer speeds are specified.

Calculating Nutrition:

- The first ingredient was used wherever a choice is given, such as ⅓ cup sour cream or plain yogurt.
- The first amount was used wherever a range is given, such as 3- to 3½-pound whole chicken.
- The first serving number was used wherever a range is given, such as 4 to 6 servings.
- "If desired" ingredients were not included.
- Only the amount of a marinade or frying oil that is absorbed was included.

America's most trusted cookbook is better than ever!

- 1,100 all-new photos, including hundreds of step-by-step images
- More than 1,500 recipes, with hundreds of inspiring variations and creative "mini" recipes for easy cooking ideas
- Brand-new features
- Gorgeous new design

Get the best edition of the *Betty Crocker Cookbook* today!

www.ingramcontent.com/pod-product-compliance
Lightning Source LLC
Chambersburg PA
CBHW071417290426
44108CB00014B/1870